# Through Every Line

## Encouragement for Troubled Times

# MIN. PATRICIA PALMER

# Introduction

If you are having trouble in your life of any kind, take heart because the word of God tells us that God is our refuge a very present help in the times of trouble. (Psalms 46:1) I have found Him to be a God that is near and not far off. One who is willing and able to help in every trail life brings. For in this life we will have tribulation; but be of good cheer for Christ has overcome the world. (John 16:33). In this book you will find poems that will encourage you to use your faith in God to overcome every obstacle that life brings; whether it be relationship problems, sickness, addictions, death or any other obstacle. Faith in Christ and what He has done for us is the glue that holds it all together. There is Victory in Jesus Christ! I hope in these pages you will find: strength, comfort, encouragement, and most of all I hope they point you to Christ, the one who is able to sustain us through all of life's ups and downs. For according to His divine power He has given us everything that pertains to life and godliness through the knowledge of Him.(2nd Peter1:3). And through all that life has to offer us, He has promised never to leave us or forsake us. As you read these poems may you find this promise to be true . . . Through Every Line.

# Contents

# *Dedication*

*This book is dedicated to the memory of my beloved parents, Rev. Moses Carstarphen, Sr. and Matilda Elizabeth Carstarphen, who instilled in me a faith and reverence for God that has helped sustain me through the trials of life. It is my prayer that this book will also be beneficial in encouraging you in your faith and reverence for God and helps sustain you through your trials in life.*

# LIFE

Is life less than what you desired or expected it to be? If so, you, like myself can probably look back at the times we chose to do other than what God had planned for us. We often times choose our way instead of His way, not realizing that God has a good plan for us (Jeremiah 29:11) and it is spelled out in His word.....

Man should not live by bread alone, but by every word that comes out of the mouth of God. (Matthew 4:4)

Until we learn this we can never effectively play the hands that life deals us . . .

# Deal Me Another Hand

I'm playing this game of life
Trying to play by the rules
But seems every time fate deals me a hand,
I loose.

I know the score keeper
He doesn't slumber nor sleep
He has ears to hear and eyes to see
Forgive me if my sin has separated me from thee
And deal me another hand
For the world is one up on me.

If we confess our sins, He is faithful and just to forgive us and
cleanse us from all unrighteousness. (I John 1:9)

# Storms of Life

I've been blown every way
I've been blown to the left
I've been blown to the right,
I've been left standing in the middle.
Now my soul is running
I've felt winds that chilled my soul,
Winds that blew so hard
I found myself  blown in the wrong direction.

. . . BUT
I will lift up mine eyes unto the hills, from whence cometh my help. My help comes from the Lord, which made heaven and earth. He will not suffer my foot to be moved: he that keeps me will not slumber. Behold, he that keeps Israel will not slumber nor sleep.
(Psalm 121: 1-4)

# A Brief Transition

Oh the years, precious years,
goes like seconds it seems
Leaving us only a short time
to chase a life time of dreams.

We're born . . . We die,
We laugh . . . We cry
Our life goes on ever changing
Our feelings and our lives ever rearranging
Cradles come rocking on the border of the grave
What can we  really promise from the beginning.....But an end

*So teach us to number our days, that we may apply our hearts unto wisdom.*
*Psalm 90:12*

# Happiness

What is Happiness?
For me it's something that use to be
A memory that fades day after day
I think it felt like sunshine
But you went away
Now I'm not warm anymore....

In all your ways acknowledge him and He will direct your path.
(Proverbs 3:6)

# *Life's Conclusion*

If there was no Night
You might not see the Light
For When Darkness Appears
Is when It shines Bright
Lighting the way to the Truth.
(I am the way, the truth, and the life, no man comes to the Father
but by me. John 14:6)

Everything that we go through in this life is for our eternal good. It may not feel good to our flesh, but if we deny our flesh and follow the Spirit of God, it will bring us from one degree of grace to another, thereby  transforming us into the image of His Son. (Roman 8:28-29)

# NATURE

The existence of God is evident in the nature around us. The bible says, The heavens declare the glory of God; and the firmaments show his handiwork. Psalm 19:1

## Where Are The Words?

Where are the words to describe our God?
Wonderful, powerful, almighty is He
All great words, but how inadequate they seem to be
I search and search, but I cannot find the words in me.
Where are the words to describe our God?
From my mind they seem to be hiding
Angels in heaven can you tell me
Where they are presiding?
Oh seraphim and cherubim do you have the list?
Or must I conclude, the words to describe Him
Just do not exist . . .

# Winter Sun

Here comes the sun,
Tripping over a frost bitten pecan tree,
Spilling through my window,
Touching me softly about the face,
Seems the hand of God has come
To stir me from my dreams
His touch warms my soul
And I greet the morning with a smile.

Bless the Lord, all his works in all places of his dominion:
bless the Lord, O my soul.
Psalm 103:22

# God Knows How to Get His Glory

Bless the Lord, O my soul, O Lord my God, thou art very great;
thou art clothed with honor and majesty.  Psalm 104:1


God knows how to get His glory,
Every time the wind bows a tree to it's God
Whether a gentle breeze blowing,
or a mighty storm from our Lord.

God knows how to get His glory,
Like when the hands of the sea
washes the face of a sandy shore
Or when the  falling rain cleans the earth once more.

God knows how to get His glory,
Every time a new born baby cries
Or when he takes his fist step,
or give his first smile.

God knows how to get His glory,
Every time the sun kisses an horizon hello
Awakening  the life here on earth below.

He knows how to get His glory,
Every time the moon pulls a dark curtain
Across the sky - called night
Or every time a twinkling star gives us light.

He knows how to get His glory,
From the fish that swim and dance in the sea
But the best way God gets His glory
Is when His love is seen in you and me.

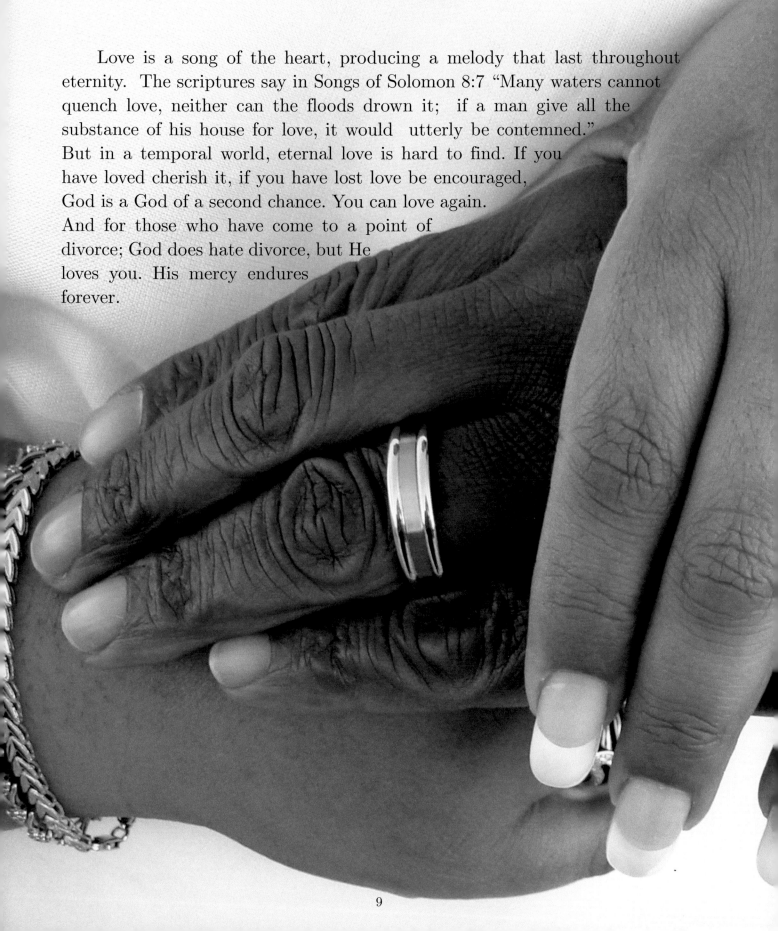

# Love Songs

Love is a song of the heart, producing a melody that last throughout eternity. The scriptures say in Songs of Solomon 8:7 "Many waters cannot quench love, neither can the floods drown it; if a man give all the substance of his house for love, it would utterly be contemned." But in a temporal world, eternal love is hard to find. If you have loved cherish it, if you have lost love be encouraged, God is a God of a second chance. You can love again. And for those who have come to a point of divorce; God does hate divorce, but He loves you. His mercy endures forever.

# Love Lost

### How Do You Make The Magic Last Forever?

How do you make the magic last forever?
Magic that makes emotions glitter and gleam
Magic, often masquerading images
From yesterday's dreams
For magic is seldom real
And it's often an elusion we feel
Through stormy words and bad times
together
Only God's love will make it last forever.

*Love bears all things, hopes all things,*
*endures all things.*
*I Corth. 13:7*

# An Elusive Dream

It seems I'm chasing an elusive dream
That glows and flickers on the horizon of my mind
And just when I think I have it clearly in sight
It drifts behind a cloud of doubt
I thought I held it in my arms
But dreams like feelings—Sometimes disappear.

*Trust in the Lord with all your heart; and lean not to your own understanding.*
*(Proverbs 3:5)*

# I Saw Love Die

*I saw Love Die:*
*First it became infected with lies*
*Distrust made it hard to breathe*
*Hurt snatched  the twinkle from Love's eyes*
*Inconsideration made Love bleed*
*Thoughtlessness knocked Love off it's feet*
*Inconsistency made Love weak*
*A loss of communication took Love's voice*
*Love being sick with fever*
*Lust became the choice*
*A loss of respect took Loves last breath*
*Shortly after Love met it's death*
*It couldn't be revived, I know, I tried*
*And now, my soul dressed in black*
*Still mourns the day I saw Love die.*

*To everything there is a season, and a time to every purpose under the heaven:*
*A time to love, and a time to hate; a time of war, and a time of peace.*
*Eccles. 3:1*

# Your Love Is Not
# What I Thought It To Be

I thought your Love was sweet,
True, not hurting, but  kind
But now I see it was a figment of my imagination
Maybe it was all in my mind.

I thought your love was a refuge from the storm
A place to go, to keep me warm
Surely, your love could do me no harm.

I was wrong it seems, now this I see
For the waves from the sea of your love is crushing me!
Your love is not what I thought it to be.

I thought your love was considerate too,
Mindful of me in all the things that you do
I was wrong, the care you had for me seems to have vanished
And the thought of me from your mind has been banished
"Let him go'" I tell myself, "Stop loving him", is my plea
Don't you see what you are doing to me
Your love is not what I thought it to be.

A love that was kind, trusting and true
Was this too much to ask of you
This is the kind of love that I sought
I was willing to pay the price
But found that it couldn't be bought
I was willing to run at it
But found it couldn't be caught.

Now disappointment darkens my heart
There is no sunshine in me
And it's all because
Your love is not what I thought it to be.

See that none render evil for evil unto any man;
but ever follow that which is good..
I Thess. 5:15

# Part II  Love Found

He heals the broken in heart, and binds up their wounds.
Psalms 147:3

## Falling In Love Again

With the feather of your smile
You tickled my heart
And love sprang a new
Love, as old as time; yet new
As the fresh morn dew

Spring is gone and summer is here
But the memory still lingers on
And instead of time diminishing it
I find it's getting stronger

It seems once again
love has taken a seat in my heart
Searching for the whole of my being
For I find that I'm only in part.

That
Your
Flower of
Love May
Grow

Song of Solomon 2:16 My beloved
is mine, and I am his.

Plant the seed of laughter in the soil of
your hearts
That your Flower of Love may grow
Give it rain, the sweet rain of kindness
So that the bud of love begins to sprout
Then let the sunshine of your smiles
Warm you through and through
So you are rooted in each others heart.
Let the sweet dew of your lips moisten your love by night
Let the warmth of your embrace make each petal glow,
A full grown flower of love, how beautiful is the sight
Take care to cherish it
So that the storms of life and the thorns of strife
Do not cause Your Love to wither and die.
But remember the laughter, the kindness,
The sweet dew of your lips, the warmth of your embrace.
The sunshine of your smiles
Remember these that your Flower of Love may grow!

# Heaven Sent

Our love was heaven sent
This I shall never forget
And these last few years of my life
Have been the best yet.
I've thought of how life would be
Without you
And it made my heart sad.
For the many wonderful things
About you, plenty outweigh
the bad.
I look forward to the
years ahead
As all our dreams
come true.
And I'm thankful
to be spending the
Rest of my life with you.

# Decision Time

There comes a time in our lives when we will be faced with a decision; to choose our own paths or to submit our will to our heavenly Father. For on our own, the cares of this life can be too cumbersome to carry, for He has told us in His word, "Cast all our cares upon him for he cares for you." (I Peter 5:7). He will deliver you. (Matthew. 11:28) Come unto me all that labor and are heavy laden, and I will give you rest.

## Let's Get High

Why do you spend money for that which is not bread? And your labor for that which satisfieth not? Harken diligently unto me, and eat that which is good, and let your soul delight itself in fatness. Isaiah 55:2

Written for Carlyle.
(Who has given his life to Christ, and now lives a sober and productive life.)

You've drunk your wine, partied every night, had a good time
But come sunrise where is your peace of mind?
You smoked your pot, loved a lot,
You'd sell your best friend to get a shot
Your body looses it's strength, your mind deteriorates,
You say, "tomorrow I'll break the habit," but will tomorrow be too late?

You've been pushed along with the crowd while your mind said nay
Somewhere Yesterday you lost your courage,
Today your self-respect and dignity,
What tomorrow, your soul in eternity?

You see yourself going downhill steady losing ground
But it's not too late the answer can still be found
Give your life to Christ, He will take and heal
Satan has you chained and bound,
But He can break the seal,
Come to Him, don't delay, the time is now to start
Everything will be all right once you're high, in God.

# Very Truly Yours

The world is asking questions
How? Why? When? Where?
Lord, I ask questions too
But while the world is searching everywhere for answers
I stand still - Looking to you
And even though our questions may seem the same
The difference is, I remain Very Truly Yours.

Discouraged and disgusted - Other ways they seek
But though I'm often cast down
I still believe - My soul you keep
And even though sometimes our questions seem the same
The difference is I remain - Very Truly Yours.

I have redeemed you, I have called you  by your name. You are mine.
Isaiah 43:1b

# If You Love Me Like You Say, Why You Do Me Like You Do?

If a man love me, he will keep my words: and my Father will love him, and we will come unto him, and make our abode with him. (John 14: 23)

If you love Me like you say,
Why you do Me like you do?
Other gods will deceive you
But My Love remains true.

I answered when you prayed
I'm the one who brought you through
I have been with you when your skies were sunny
And when life's sorrows made you blue
If you love Me like you say,
Why you do Me like you do?

If you suffer with Me you shall reign with Me
I have even prepared a place for you,
That where I am you can be there too
If you love Me like you say,
Why you do Me like you do?

Deny yourself and this world too
My love, My peace, My joy, and self-control pursue
Follow after Me, for My Spirit is in you
If you love Me like you say,
Why you do Me like you do?

If you love Me like you say,
Why you do Me like you do?
I'm the one who suffered, bled, and died for you
Pledge Me your love and remain true.

# The Wise Shall Understand

Many shall be purified, made white, and refined, but the
wicked shall do wickedly; and none of the wicked shall
understand, but the wise shall understand. (Daniel 12:10)

The rain falls down upon the land
So that a flower may grow
Or a blade of grass may stand
All of your ways are so high, so grand
Sometimes they seem hard to understand
So Lord, hold me by the hand.

The hurt, the pain done by evil man
I must turn the cheek again
But in our lives you make, you mold
You are the Overseer of our soul
Life has hills, valleys, and level plains
On this journey, just hold me by the hand.

I remember nights I had to cry
Not knowing that you were purging to purify
To do your will, not that of man
With your strength I know I can,
If you hold me by the hand.

The end of all things are close at hand
There is so much trouble in the land
Scale so small, or oh so grand
Only what's done for Christ will stand,
So Lord, hold me by the hand.

You suffered, bled, and died, for man
May your glory be revealed in me again
As I walk in your will, I've grown to understand
That I am a partaker of your suffering
I am wiser, now I understand.

# Prayer & Praise

If we draw close to God He will draw close to us. (James 4:8) The bible says, " the effectual fervent prayer of a righteous man availed much. (James 5:16b). And it is true that when praises go up, blessings come down.

## Pray Again

(Roman 12:12 Rejoicing in hope, patient in tribulation,
continuing steadfastly in prayer.)

Prayer is a supernatural connection

The key to God's supreme affection
For no prayer is whispered in vain
And with prayer things do change,
So pray again.

Prayer is the door to God through His Son
It is the force that keeps us moving on
Prayer will guide us in the right direction
Giving us God's mighty protection
Prayer is the thing that moves trouble,
heartache and pain
So pray again.

Prayer lifts us from valley so low to mountain so high
Prayer moves God's hand to wipe tears when we cry
Prayer is the thing that makes a sad heart sing
So pray again.

# Call On Him

*The righteous cry out, and the Lord hears,*
*and delivers them out of all their troubles. (Psalm 34:17)*

*Call on Him, He will hear your prayer*
*In times of trouble He'll be there*
*He has promised not to leave you and He never will*
*Call on Him*
*He's waiting for you still.*

*With outstretched arms He will take and comfort you*
*You are still His child, He will see you through*
*When your way gets dark and it seem so very dim*
*He still answers prayer*
*Just call on Him.*

*Even when you can't trace His hands*
*In His word you can trace His heart*
*He is right there with you as He was from the start*
*He's been your Father, your Guide, and your Friend,*
*Call On Him.*

# A Prayer for The Country

2 Chronicles 7:14  If my people, which are called by my name, shall humble themselves, and pray, and seek my face, and turn from their wicked ways; then will I hear from heaven, and will forgive their sin, and will heal their land.

*Leader of Leaders, God of all might*
*Teach us, Lead us, and show us what's right*
*Shining Light, that leads to Truth everlasting*
*Upon you now our failures we're casting*
*Take them and make them a future success*
*With your everlasting love our Country do bless.*

*Start with the home, woman and man*
*And with your divine guidance show us your plan*
*Children, so innocent so free from care*
*Tomorrow's great leaders are brewing there*

*Bless us dear Master; your bride to be*
*Your called out believers working for Thee*
*Without spot or wrinkle, the Church stands adorned*
*Until the Bridegroom comes that glorious morn.*

*Look upon our country, and heal it's deep wounds,*
*For only your grace can rid us from doom*
*We search for Thee now, for now Lord we must*
*Have mercy on us, for, " In God We Trust."*

# Grateful Praise

*Offer to God thanksgiving;*
*and pay your vows to the most high. (Psalms 50:14)*

*Our hearts are full of praise and special thanks to Thee*
*Most of all for the work you did on Calvary*
*We thank you for our home, our friends, our family*
*Thank you for the portion of strength given to serve Thee*
*Thank you for our food, our clothes, and shoes for our feet*
*For all these things we give grateful praise to thee*
*We thank you for the good times when we can see the sun*
*And we thank you for the bad times when the rain has come.*

*We thank, you for the beauty of nature you have given to enjoy*
*We thank you for hearing prayers, by which, your help we employ*
*Thank you for your Grace and Mercy that stays at our back*
*To keep our feet from falling, to give us what we lack*
*We even thank you for every enemy that kept us looking up*
*For we found how sweet you were after tasting their*
*bitter cup*
*We thank you for the bad times and the good*
*times too*
*We thank you for the plenty and We*
*thank you for the few*
*Lord, you are Glorious and Wonderful,*
*you are our Heavenly King*
*And one day we'll be able to*
*praise you right*
*When throughout eternity*
*we shall sing.*

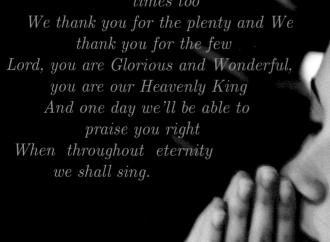

25

*Father*

Will you comfort me when the evening comes?
May I lay my head on your shoulders,
When loneliness plays hid and seek with my soul,
When the darkness stripes me
And I stand before myself
Minute in the scheme of things
Searching for a moment in time?

Roman 8:15  For ye  have not received the spirit of bondage again to fear; but
ye have received the Spirit of adoption, whereby we cry, Abba, Father.

## (A Prayer)
# Be My Vindicator

Dearly beloved, avenge not
yourselves, but rather give place
unto wrath: for it is written,
Vengeance is mine; I will repay,
saith the Lord. (Roman 12:19)

Lord you're my vindicator
You're my way maker
Come what may
You will save the day
For You will build a fence
All around me when I pray
For You are my defense
Each and everyday.

You're my vindicator
Your strength you will show
The fires will not burn me
Nor waters overflow
My faith looks up to Thee
Where ever I may go
Defend and uphold me
Now and forever more.

# Death Calls

## Dust To Dust

(And now I sleep in the dust; and thou shall seek me in the morning, but I shall not be found. Job 7:21)

Mother earth-calling us back from whence we came
Dust to dust, our mortal frame
Each new wrinkle, each passing year
Draws us constantly nearer and nearer.

For we are all but grains of sand
Formed by God into man
These mortal bodies all prone to decay
Will one day heed the call
And all pass away...

Man is like unto vanity; his days are a shadow that passes away.
Psalm 144:4

Blessed is the dead that die in the Lord, for so shall they ever be with the Lord.

Death is never easy because it separates us from our loved ones; but the bible tells us not sorrow as others who have no hope. (Thess. 4:13)

# In Your time of Sorrow

(IPeter 5:7)  Cast your cares upon Him: for He cares for you.

He that clothe the lilies of the fields
That soon wither away,
He that feeds a sparrow from day to day
Will He not heal your broken heart
When you pray?

When you call He will surely come,
For even the hairs upon your head are numbered
Each and every one
You are precious in His sight
And He will hold you up
With His strength, with His might.

# In Memory of :

## CATLIN SANDERS, July 12, 1994
## (And All Stillborn Babies)

*God's Peculiar Treasure*
*For if we believe that Jesus died and rose again,*
*even so them also which sleep in Jesus will God bring*
*with him.*
*I Thessalonians 4:14*

*They must have shone with an inner beauty*
*That was too bright for this dark world*
*One that only God Himself could appreciate*
*Jewels too precious to be given, so God Himself*
*Stored them in His own special treasure*
*And has hidden them on high*
*Where they cannot be touched by the evils of this world.*
*And when Christ returns*
*We will all be changed*
*Into a glory liken unto them*
*And we too, will be reunited with them*
*As part of God's Peculiar Treasure.*

# It's All Right To Cry

And God shall wipe away all tears from their eyes; and there shall be no more death, neither sorrow, nor crying, neither shall there be any more pain; for the former things are passed away.  (Rev. 21:4 )

*It's all right to cry, for every tear will be a jewel*
*That adorns your heavenly crown*
*Every heartache will be turned to praise*
*When you gather around His throne*
*God will make right every evil done*
*He will wipe away your tears*
*Each and everyone.*

*It's all right to cry for every one of your prayers*
*In a bottle He holds*
*And every test of faith will be proven pure gold*
*Every goodbye will be turned to howdy*
*In that homeland in the sky*
*But while we are down here, It's all right to cry.*
*For when all is said and done*
*He will wipe away our tears*
*Each and everyone.*

*And He said unto me, Write:  for these words are true and faithful.  It is done.*
*I am Alpha and Omega, the beginning and the end.  (Rev. 21:  5b&6a  )*

# Encouragement

*For it is better, if the will of God be so, that ye suffer for well doing, than for evil doing.*
*(I Peter 3:17 )*

# Encouragement During Your Trying Time

I was sorry to hear about the breaking of your heart
The hurting within, the pulling apart
But you are not alone; you have an eternal friend
And He knows how to put a broken heart back together again.

If you have done all you can
Rest that it is all a part of His plan,
Even if you don't understand
For it is true that trials come to make us strong
That we must do good even when wronged.

And when it is all over, you will see
That it has worked for your good, eternally
Though the outer man would have suffered, but not in vain
The inner man will have withstood for a greater gain.

Hold up your shield of faith
For this battle you too will win
And you will hear God's voice say.
"Well done thou good and faithful servant," at the end.

Reference: I Peter 3:14-18

# Remember Whose You Are

*You comprehend my path and my lying down,*
*and are acquainted with all my ways. (Psalm 139:3)*

No matter where you go, remember whose you are
Where ever life takes you, whether near or far
The times that you are home, or the times that you are gone
You are not your mother's nor your father's
You are not even your own
For you have been bought with a price
The contract of your purchase written in the blood of Christ.

So, no matter where you go, remember whose you are
Deny even yourself and take up your cross
There will bc many ways presented, resist them,
no matter how hard
For Jesus is the only way that will lead you to God
Psalm 34:12-13 says if you want many days
And you want to see good
Keep your tongue from evil and deceit like you should.

Lean not to your own understanding,
Ask God which way you should go
Pray and read his word, and His will to you He will show
He has forgiven you for all sins, and still calls you His friend
So no matter where you go, remember whose you are,
And He will remember you at the judgment bar.

# God Has Not Forgotten You!

*The Lord also will be a refuge for the oppressed, a refuge in times of trouble.*
*And they that know your name will put their trust in you. (Psalm 9: 9-10)*

The Lord won't cast you asunder
He'll hold you up, for He's still a mighty wonder
No matter how hard it seems, He did not make a blunder
When things within and out seem to crumble
Sometimes even causing you to stumble
He'll  still help you if you're humble.

No matter how it seems, seek Him
He remembers your dreams
Your enemies may plot, they may scheme
But, you'll come out on top if on Him you continue to lean.

For He has not forgotten those who seek His Holy face
He'll bring you through by His amazing Grace
Remember what He has already brought you through
You are still His child, He has not forgotten you.

# As You Are Starting Over

Forgetting  those things that are behind, and reaching forth unto those things which are before, I press toward the mark for the prize of the high calling of God in  Jesus Christ.
(Phil. 3:13-14.)

Starting over is not an easy thing to do
But it's not hard if you ask God to go before you
For He that clothe the lilies of the fields
That soon wither away
He that feeds a sparrow from day to day
Will surely hear you when you pray.

When you call He will surely come
For even the hairs upon your head
Are numbered, each and every one
You are precious in His sight
And He will hold you up
With His strength, with His might.

# Not Condoned, But Not Condemned.

When Jesus had lifted up himself, and saw no one but the woman, he said unto her, Woman, where are those that accuse you? Has no man condemned you? Neither do I condemn you, go and sin no more. (John 8:10,11B)

Young girls laying it all down
For a promise, for a thrill
Not even using a condom, not even using a pill
Not realizing that they are starting a struggle
That is all up hill.

Seems everything's coming a loose at the seams
Broken promises, broken dreams
Even a broken heart.
But God will mend,
Forgive you for your sins,
Make you whole again.
For God still loves you so,
Go and sin no more.

# Be Still Fainting Heart

*Wait on the Lord: be of good courage,*
*and he shall strengthen thine heart: wait, I say, on the Lord. (Psalm 27:14 )*

*Be still  fainting heart*
*Though nights, are long and dark*
*Submit to God's chastening rod*
*That you may be brought into obedience to your lord*
*Trusting His strength as on life's weary road you trod*
*Be still fainting heart*
*And know that God is God!*

*Be still fainting heart*
*Remember what he has already brought you through*
*How many times*
*Will he have to prove his love for you*
*Read His words,*
*And listen for the wisdom He imparts*
*Rely on His Grace as you did from the start*
*Be still  fainting heart,*
*And know that God is God!*

# My Faith Looks Up to Thee

Unto thee I lift up my eyes, O thou that dwellest in the heavens.
Psalm 123:1

When bitter words, like a piercing sword
Have deeply wounded me
Lord, my faith looks up to thee,
When disappointment like a river floods my soul
And the way I can't plainly see
Lord, my faith looks up to thee,
For I know that for the hurt and pain
You will give me peace
When my faith looks up to thee.

# The Barren Heart

*Man shall not live by bread alone,*
*but by every word that proceeds out of the mouth of God. (Matthew 4:4)*

*Thirsty and hungry is the heart*
*That has not the word of God hidden in it . . .*

**The Word of God Is:**
***Light*** *in darkness*
*That a lost soul might be saved,*
***Comfort*** *in Grief*
*when death has taken*
*Our loved ones to the grave,*
***Hope*** *in Distress*
*That says that we can go on,*
***Strength*** *in weakness*
*When our strength is gone,*
***Health*** *in sickness*
*No matter how we feel,*
***Faith*** *to know that God is real,*
***Love,*** *in it God's face we can see,*
*It is our **Guide** from here to eternity.*

*(Heaven and earth shall pass away,*
*but my words shall not pass away.  Mark 31:31 )*

39

# Redeemed

Buda, Muhammad, Krishna, were all good men; but they did not do what Jesus did, neither did they claim to. No one but Jesus gave his life as a sacrifice in death, then rose again the third day, and has gone to prepare a place for us on high, and has given us the promise that he will return again and receive us unto himself, and so shall we ever be with the lord.

Jesus
That at the name of Jesus every knee should bow,
And every tongue should confess that Jesus is Lord.
(Phil. 2 10-11)

Who else has suffered,
Bled and died?
Who else has come to
Live  inside?
Who else has prepared a place for us on High?

Who else has gotten up from the dead?
Who else did it just like He said?
Who else gave defeated man victory instead?

No other name under the sun.
Has done what he has done?
No, not one.

# One Night With The King

Who is this King of glory? The Lord of hosts, He is the King of glory.
(Psalm 24:10)

It only takes a night with The King to have a new start
One Night to give Him the throne of your heart
You've ruled long enough, give Him the reign
You will see things turn around, things will change
He'll take off the  raggedness of your sin,
That you're clothed in
And clothed you in the royalty of His Righteousness
A new life to begin
"One Night With The King," can change everything
A new walk, A new talk will be seen
If you spend "One Night with The King."

It only takes a night with The King to have a new start
One Night to give Him the throne of your heart
In His presence you'll find that true Love abounds
And you'll be glad to spread this Love you've found
"One Night With The King"
And He will change your name
One night with Him and the things
Of this world will all seem vain
Now Peace and Joy you'll have forever around His throne
Now one day heaven will be your home
With Him  through out eternity you will reign
All because you decided to spend "One Night with The King."

# Thank You for Your Blood

*Much more then, having now been justified by His blood,*
*we shall be saved from wrath through Him. (Roman 5:9)*

We remember Calvary
How you hung there on a tree
That day mercy did abound
When your blood came streaming down.

You were the King of Kings
And they gave you a crown of thorns
The same hands that healed the sick
Were pierced, tattered, and torn.

So Lord, we thank you for your blood
That you shed because of love
You came and died for our sins
So that we might live again.

We remember how they thought you were doomed
And laid you in a borrowed tomb
They did not realize
That three days later You would rise

Now we can sing,
"Oh grave where is your victory, death where is your sting?"
Christ lives, So we can live eternally
We now have the victory!

So Lord, we thank you for your blood
That you shed because of love
Your precious life you did give
So that sinful man could live.

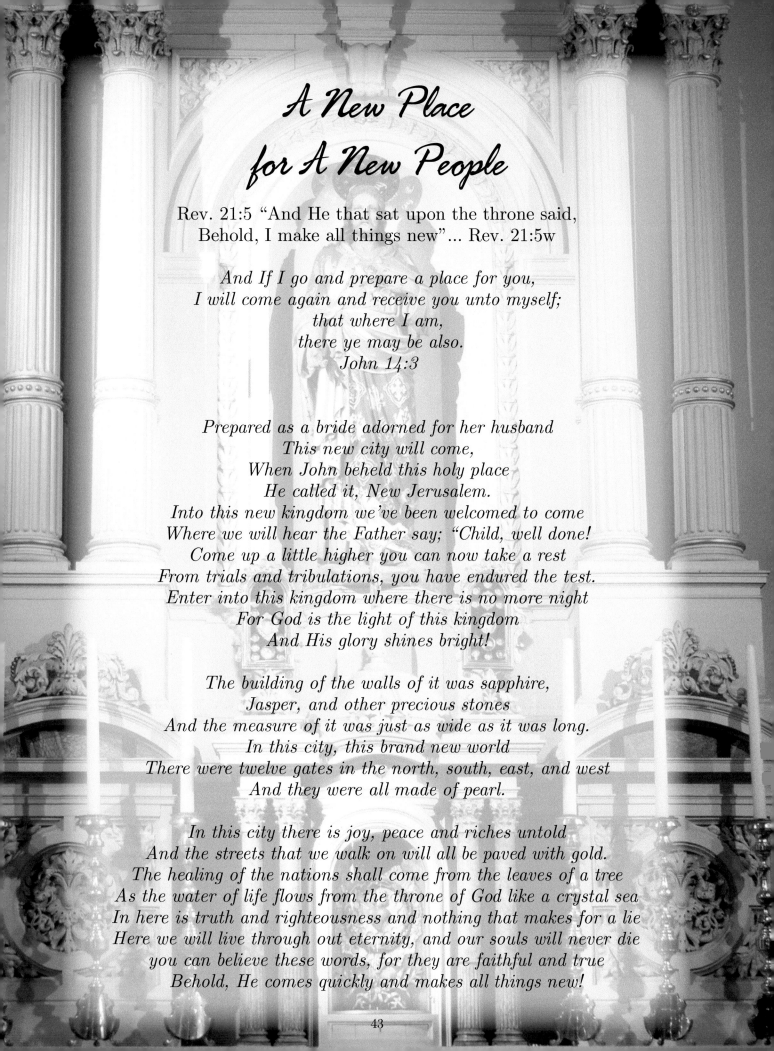

# A New Place
# for A New People

Rev. 21:5 "And He that sat upon the throne said,
Behold, I make all things new"... Rev. 21:5w

*And If I go and prepare a place for you,*
*I will come again and receive you unto myself;*
*that where I am,*
*there ye may be also.*
*John 14:3*

*Prepared as a bride adorned for her husband*
*This new city will come,*
*When John beheld this holy place*
*He called it, New Jerusalem.*
*Into this new kingdom we've been welcomed to come*
*Where we will hear the Father say; "Child, well done!*
*Come up a little higher you can now take a rest*
*From trials and tribulations, you have endured the test.*
*Enter into this kingdom where there is no more night*
*For God is the light of this kingdom*
*And His glory shines bright!*

*The building of the walls of it was sapphire,*
*Jasper, and other precious stones*
*And the measure of it was just as wide as it was long.*
*In this city, this brand new world*
*There were twelve gates in the north, south, east, and west*
*And they were all made of pearl.*

*In this city there is joy, peace and riches untold*
*And the streets that we walk on will all be paved with gold.*
*The healing of the nations shall come from the leaves of a tree*
*As the water of life flows from the throne of God like a crystal sea*
*In here is truth and righteousness and nothing that makes for a lie*
*Here we will live through out eternity, and our souls will never die*
*you can believe these words, for they are faithful and true*
*Behold, He comes quickly and makes all things new!*

# GOD SENT HIS SON

For God so loved the world, that he gave his only begotten Son, that whosoever believeth in him should not perish, but have everlasting life. John 3:16

God sent His Son, clothed in a body of flesh
To leave His throne in glory to die an undeserved death
Jesus bear our sins and died on Calvary
If there was no Jesus, where would we all be?
Jesus, the Word, that came from the heart of God
To die that you and I may have an unmerited reward
For it's nothing that we've done, nothing we could do,
But he paid the price of salvation that it may be free to me and you.
Not born among the Jews, not born among the chosen were we,
But God the Father loved us, and He has set us free.
The law is just, but cruel, strong, but through the flesh made weak
But Jesus Christ has made away and we have but to seek,
You hear voices crying justice, justice here, justice now,
But through, the blood of Jesus, mercy shall abound.
Jesus, precious Jesus, praise, thanks to thee,
Who saved our souls from hell's fiery eternity
And has given us a seat on the right side of Thee
It makes me stop and wonder, deep inside of me.
If there was no Jesus where would we all be?

*Prayer of Faith*
I admit that I am a sinner. I accept and believe that Jesus died and rose to life again that I might be forgiven of my sins. I now receive Him as my personal Savior. I turn now from my sins and commit my life to Him.

Printed in the United States
By Bookmasters